SPEED MACHINES

ATVs

BY MATT SCHEFF

SportsZone

An Imprint of Abdo Publishing
www.abdopublishing.com

www.abdopublishing.com

Published by Abdo Publishing, a division of ABDO, PO Box 398166,
Minneapolis, Minnesota 55439. Copyright © 2015 by Abdo Consulting Group,
Inc. International copyrights reserved in all countries. No part of this
book may be reproduced in any form without written permission from the
publisher. SportsZone™ is a trademark and logo of Abdo Publishing.

Printed in the United States of America, North Mankato, Minnesota
082014
012015

THIS BOOK CONTAINS
RECYCLED MATERIALS

Cover Photo: Shutterstock Images
Interior Photos: Shutterstock Images, 1, 8-9, 14-15, 22-23; Daily Free Press,
Zach Frailey/AP Images, 4-5, 6-7; Richard Hamilton Smith/Corbis, 10-11;
Scott Nelson/AP Images, 12-13; Dmitry Naumov/Shutterstock Images, 16-17;
Mesaib Daily News, Mark Sauer/AP Images, 18-19; Dr. Ajay Kumar Singh/
Shutterstock Images, 19; Art Konovalov/Shutterstock Images, 20-21, 26-27,
31; Breck Smither/AP Images, 24-25; Rex Features/AP Images, 28-29

Editor: Chrös McDougall
Series Designer: Nikki Farinella

Library of Congress Control Number: 2014944185

Cataloging-in-Publication Data
Scheff, Matt.
 ATVs / Matt Scheff.
   p. cm. -- (Speed machines)
ISBN 978-1-62403-608-8 (lib. bdg.)
Includes bibliographical references and index.
1. All terrain vehicles--Juvenile literature.   I. Title.
629.22--dc23
                                                  2014944185

CONTENTS

THE FINAL TURN

Dirt sprays in the air as a neon-green all-terrain
vehicle (ATV) speeds over the course. Its driver is
leading the ATV Motocross (ATVMX) race. But a bright
red ATV follows close behind. The seats rattle and
shake as the engines roar. Both drivers sail over a big
jump. The finish line is within sight.

ATV drivers begin a race.

FAST FACT

ATVMX races are held on tracks. The races last 15 minutes followed by two additional laps.

FAST FACT

Cross-country ATV races take place on natural terrain, such as sand or woodlands. They usually last less than two hours.

The bright red ATV takes the lead.

The drivers lean into the final turn. They can feel every bump and dip in the track as their tires dig into the dirt. Just then, the driver of the bright red ATV speeds up. Meanwhile, the neon-green ATV is going too fast. Its rear tires begin to slip and lose their grip. The bright red vehicle cruises past and crosses the finish line in first place.

THE HISTORY OF ATVs

People have been building vehicles to run off-road for more than 100 years. But the modern ATV really began to take its shape in the early 1970s. That's when Honda released the US90 model. It was the first three-wheeled ATV. The US90 had huge balloon tires and sat high off the ground.

The first ATVs weren't as powerful as today's models.

In the early 1980s, Honda and other ATV builders made some changes. They ditched the balloon tires. Instead, they added smaller wheels with strong suspension systems. These ATVs sat closer to the ground. They were faster and more stable. Around this time, Suzuki introduced a four-wheeled ATV, the LT125 QuadRunner. ATV builders stopped making three-wheeled vehicles during the 1980s. They found that four-wheel ATVs were much safer.

A three-wheeled ATV rides over sand during the 1980s.

ATVs soon branched out into two types, sport and utility. Sport ATVs are lightweight and built for speed. These ATVs are used mainly for fun and for racing. Utility ATVs are larger, heavier, and usually slower. Utility ATVs are working vehicles. They can tow trailers and haul loads.

US Army Special Forces soldiers ride ATVs in Afghanistan.

FAST FACT

Some utility ATVs have six wheels
instead of four.

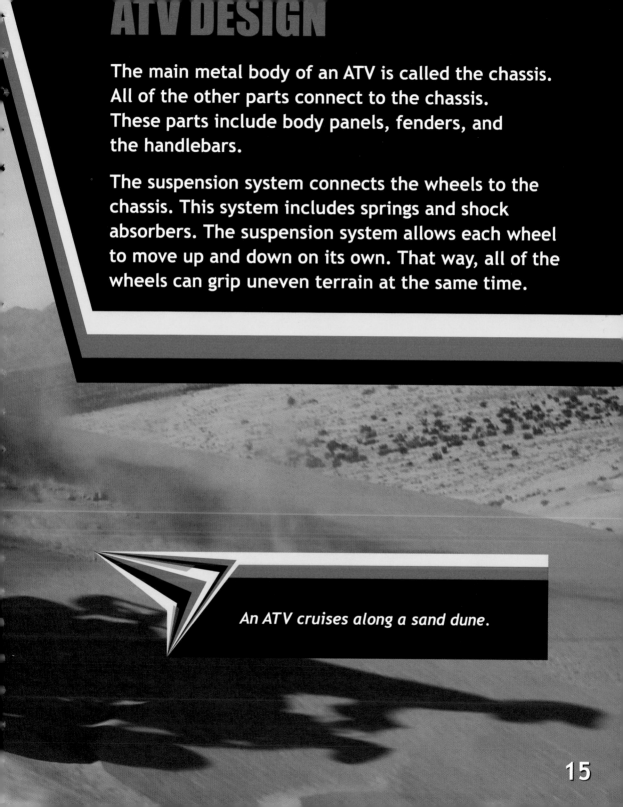

ATV DESIGN

The main metal body of an ATV is called the chassis. All of the other parts connect to the chassis. These parts include body panels, fenders, and the handlebars.

The suspension system connects the wheels to the chassis. This system includes springs and shock absorbers. The suspension system allows each wheel to move up and down on its own. That way, all of the wheels can grip uneven terrain at the same time.

An ATV cruises along a sand dune.

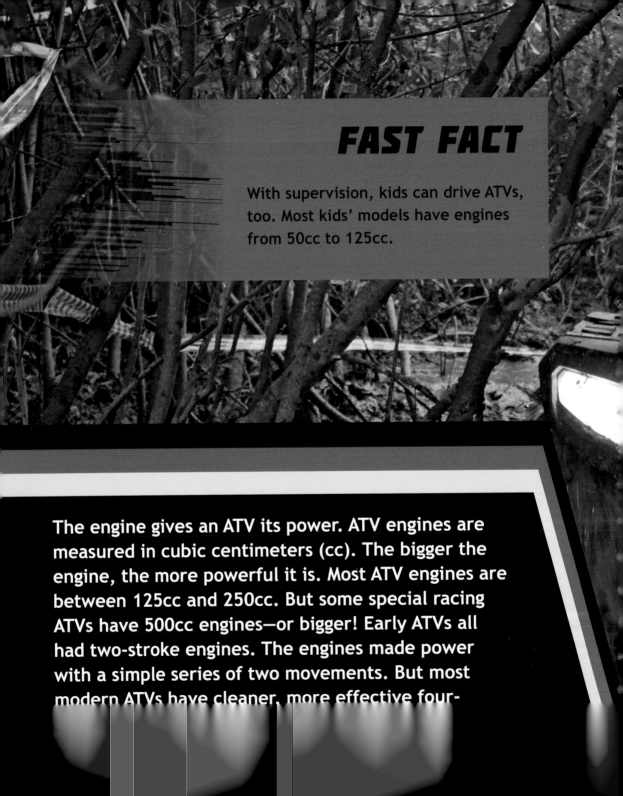

The engine gives an ATV its power. ATV engines are measured in cubic centimeters (cc). The bigger the engine, the more powerful it is. Most ATV engines are between 125cc and 250cc. But some special racing ATVs have 500cc engines—or bigger! Early ATVs all had two-stroke engines. The engines made power with a simple series of two movements. But most modern ATVs have cleaner, more effective four-

An ATV drives through a deep swamp.

ATVs drive down a path in Minnesota's Iron Range.

ATV tires have deep tread.

ATVs need tires with deep tread to give them the best grip. Basic all-terrain tires can handle most any surface. But drivers can use special tires that better grip mud or sand.

An ATV's transmission brings the power from the engine to the wheels. Many sport ATVs have two-wheel drive. Utility ATVs use four-wheel drive. Four-wheel drive ATVs can better handle mud, sand, and other off-trail conditions.

PHOTO DIAGRAM

1. Helmet
2. Gloves
3. Boots
4. Body
5. Tires
6. Suspension system
7. Handlebars

ATVs ON THE LOOSE

ATVs have all kinds of uses. Hunters drive ATVs through forests and over rocky hills and mountains. In the winter, some people drive ATVs onto frozen lakes to go ice fishing. Thrill-seekers use ATVs to climb huge sand dunes. Others just like to take their ATVs out for a joyride on trails.

An ATV rider makes his way through a snow-covered field.

Police officers use ATVs to patrol railroad tracks.

Many people use ATVs for work. Construction workers take ATVs to hard-to-reach sites. Park rangers ride ATVs to get around state and national parks. Some farmers and ranchers rely on ATVs to get from field to field and to herd cattle. Some people even add snowplow blades to the front of their ATVs. This allows the ATVs to clear snow from narrow spots like streets, sidewalks, and driveways.

FAST FACT

A new class of vehicle is the utility task vehicle (UTV). A UTV is bigger and more powerful than an ATV. UTVs can seat up to four people.

FAST FACT

Chad Wienen is one of the top ATV racers in the world. He won the top ATVMX championship in both 2012 and 2013.

COMPETITION

Many people who own ATVs like to race them. Drivers of any skill level can compete in off-road races around the world. Some races are just for kids. The top ATV drivers race specialized racing machines in ATVMX. Drivers speed around courses with sharp turns, big jumps, and bumpy straightaways.

ATVs drive around a dirt track.

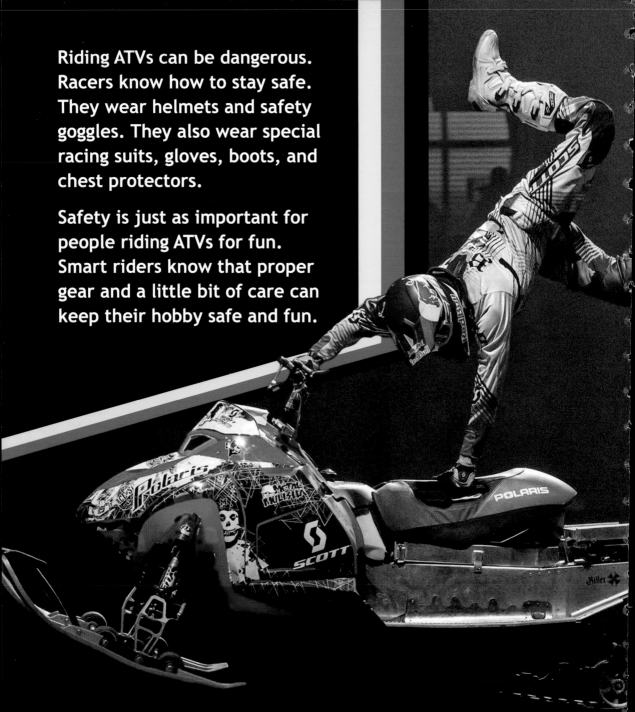

Riding ATVs can be dangerous. Racers know how to stay safe. They wear helmets and safety goggles. They also wear special racing suits, gloves, boots, and chest protectors.

Safety is just as important for people riding ATVs for fun. Smart riders know that proper gear and a little bit of care can keep their hobby safe and fun.

A snowmobile rider and an ATV rider perform tricks together at a Nitro Circus show.

GLOSSARY

balloon tires
A type of wide, fat, low-pressure tire that was common on early ATVs.

chassis
The main metal frame of an ATV.

fender
A body panel that covers part of a vehicle, such as a wheel, to protect it from collisions.

motocross
A type of race held on dirt courses with lots of turns and jumps.

stroke
A movement of an engine's cylinders to burn fuel. ATV engines can run on a series of two strokes or a series of four strokes.

suspension system
The system of shock absorbers and springs that connects an ATV's chassis to its wheels.

terrain
The shape of natural land.

tread
A series of bumps and grooves that helps a tire grip a surface such as dirt or mud.

utility
Built for doing work.

FOR MORE INFORMATION

Books

David, Jack. *ATVs*. Minneapolis: Bellwether Media, 2008.

Kosara, Tori. *Amazing Motorcycles; Awesome ATVs*.
New York: Scholastic, 2013.

Websites

To learn more about Speed Machines,
visit **booklinks.abdopublishing.com**. These links
are routinely monitored and updated to provide
the most current information available.

INDEX

ABOUT THE AUTHOR

Matt Scheff is a freelance author and lifelong motor sports fan living in Minnesota.